pomeran

understanding and
caring for your dog

Written by
Jacqueline Gray

Pomeranian

pomeranian

understanding and
caring for your dog

Written by
Jacqueline Gray

Pet Book Publishing Company,

The Old Hen House, St Martin's Farm, Zeals, Warminster, Wiltshire, BA12 6NZ

Printed and bound in South Korea through Pacom.

Every reasonable care has been taken in the compilation of this publication. The Publisher and Author cannot accept liability for any loss, damage, injury or death resulting from the keeping of Pomeranians by user(s) of this publication, or from the use of any materials, equipment, methods or information recommended in this publication or from any errors or omissions that may be found in the text of this publication or that may occur at a future date, except as expressly provided by law.

The 'he' pronoun is used throughout this book instead of the rather impersonal 'it', however no gender bias is intended.

ISBN: 978-1-906305-72-7
ISBN: 1-906305-72-2

Acknowledgements

The publishers would like to thank the following for help with photography: Bill and Jean Stone (Billijees).

Contents

Introducing the Pomeranian

Bright, alert, loyal and loving, the Pomeranian is the ideal companion dog – and he knows it!

The Pomeranian is among the smallest of dog breeds – but no one told him that. He is the perfect miniature dog, yet he has a huge personality. He thrives on being the centre of attention, and if your focus drifts away from him, he will be quick to remind you of his presence with an imperious bark!

Physical characteristics

The Pomeranian is known as the puffball of the canine world because of his round shape and luxuriant coat. He has very decided features; a small fox-like head, dark eyes with a lively, mischievous expression, a compact body, and a tail that curls over to lie flat on his back.

However, his most outstanding feature is his coat, which comes in a variety of stunning colors. The texture of the coat is of particular significance. Bred down from the

larger spitz breeds of the North, he retains a coat that would protect him from extreme cold. He has a soft, dense undercoat, and a harsh-textured topcoat that prevents the undercoat from getting wet. It is the harsh, stand-off quality of the topcoat that helps to give the Pomeranian his distinctive round shape.

The question of size

Pomeranians weight between 3 and 7lb (1.3-3.1 kg). Height is not stipulated, but they range between 7 and 11 inches (18-28cm). Smaller dogs are preferred in the show ring, and larger dogs are more suitable as pets. However, there is a fashion for breeding 'teapot Pomeranians', with breeders striving to produce tiny Pomeranians as handbag dogs.

This is not in the best interests of the breed. Smaller Poms experience problems with whelping and, although small in size, the Pom should be a robust dog capable of leading an active life.

Temperament

The Pomeranian is out-going, lively and intelligent – this is a dog that lives life to the full. He is the perfect people dog, with a loving and affectionate nature, and a happy-go-lucky approach to life.

He is a natural watchdog, and he takes this role very seriously. He is always on the alert and will give a warning bark when visitors are close by – long before you are aware of their approach. But when he meets new people, after an initial check, the Pom is the friendliest of dogs and will soon be trying to hop into the nearest lap!

Do not make the mistake of treating your Pomeranian like a lapdog. There is no doubt that he enjoys his creature comforts, and is always ready for a cuddle, but he also wants to be treated like a proper dog. He has a brain and he likes to use it, so mental stimulation is essential for this dainty little dog.

Companion dog

The Pomeranian is a very versatile breed and will suit a variety of different owners. He will live happily in the town or the country, and will be equally content in an apartment or in a mansion.

What he does need is company. The Pomeranian is a Toy dog bred specifically to be a companion, so he will be miserable if he has to spend lengthy periods on his own. He is the perfect breed for people getting on in years as he does not require extensive exercise, but he will also fit in with a more active household.

The Pom does get on well with children, as long as both parties learn mutual respect. However, he is better suited to older children who will have a better understanding of his needs.

Pomeranian (right) with a Yorkshire Terrier.

Living with other dogs

The Pomeranian enjoys the company of other dogs, particularly his own kind. Possibly harking back to his distant ancestors, the Pom enjoys being in a pack, and as Poms are so collectible, you may soon find yourself with a mini tribe, all vying for your attention.

Trainability

You may think you can get away with minimal training if you have a dog the size of a Pomeranian. But this is emphatically not the case. The Pom is as bright as a button, and he will twist you round his little finger in no time. He can be quite demanding, and so he needs an owner he can respect.

The ideal owner will give the Pom a chance to use his brain, teaching him basic obedience, and maybe adding in a few party tricks so he can show off when you have visitors. The Pom also needs consistent handling so he knows what is, and is not, allowed. In this way, you will rear a Pomeranian that understand his place in your family.

Life expectancy

In common with most Toy breeds, the Pomeranian has a good life expectancy, and, with luck, most will reach double figures, many surviving well into their teens.

Tracing back in time

The Pomeranian is a member of the spitz family, and dogs of this type have an ancient history dating back some 10,000 years. They had to be tough enough to withstand the harsh climate, and with the strength and endurance to pull sleds. Some dogs were used for hunting, and they also played a role guarding livestock from predators.

Of course, these working dogs were far bigger than the Pom, but the breed still retains some characteristics from his Nordic cousins. He has an abundant coat, with a thick woolly undercoat, which would have protected him from the worst of the weather, and his small, erect ears are fine-tuned for hearing the approach of danger.

The spitz breeds

Spitz breeds include the Japanese Akita, Alaskan Malamute, Samoyed, Chow Chow, Finnish Spitz and German Spitz.

All spitz breeds share the following characteristics:

- Tail that is carried over the back.

- Erect, pricked ears.

- Thick, dense, double waterproof coat.

Into Europe

At some point in their history, the spitz breeds were transported to Europe, most commonly along the southern coast of the Baltic sea. This region, which lies between eastern Germany and northern Poland, was known as Pomerania, and it is from here that the Pom gets his name.

Pomerania, meaning 'of the sea', was a busy sea-trading area, and the dogs from the north thrived in their new home. The smaller dogs were particular favorites, and over a period of time, a small type was produced, although it was still ten times larger than the modern Pom!

Japanese Akita: Despite differences in size, the spitz breeds bear a strong resemblance to each other.

There is evidence that the new spitz breed was taken further afield into the warmer climates of the south. In Greece, jars and jugs, depicting spitz-like companion dogs, have been found, dating back to 200BC. They were also featured on artefacts found in the pharaohs' tombs of ancient Egypt.

Royal favor

Many of our Toy dogs have strong links with royalty, and the Pomeranian is no exception.

George III acceded to the British throne in 1760 when he was just 22 and still unmarried. Following a hurried search to find a suitable wife, he was married to Charlotte of Mecklenburg-Streliz, whom he first met on his wedding day.

Charlotte would have known of the dogs from Pomerania as she spent her childhood in the bordering region of Mecklenburg. Once she was settled in England, she sent for two dogs – Phoebe and Mercury – and this was the start of the breed's development in England.

We have pictorial evidence of these two dogs as they featured in a number of paintings by the famous artist, Sir Thomas Gainsborough. They were clearly much bigger than the Pomeranian we know today, probably weighing around 30lb (13.6kg), but they

Facing page: The smallest dogs were selected for breeding with the aim of producing a diminutive Toy dog.

have the distinctive heavy coat, pricked ears, and tail carried over the back.

As the breed became established in England, there was a growing interest in developing a smaller dog. Occasionally a 'dwarf' was born in a litter that was about one-third the size of his siblings. These dwarfs, known as 'sports' weighed around 12lb (5.4kg) in adulthood, and were much sought after by breed enthusiasts. Soon they were being used in breeding programs with the deliberate aim of producing smaller-sized Poms.

Developing the breed

In 1859 there is the first record of a Pomeranian competing in a dog show. A 'Pomeranian Fox Dog' was entered in the Foreign Dogs Non-sporting category at the UK's Birmingham show.

In the first Kennel Club Stud Book (1862-1873) there are several Pomeranians listed, including Alba, Blanco, Carlo and Charlie. At this stage, dogs were mostly red, cream or biscuit in color; blacks were very rare.

But it was from 1888 that the breed really took off and, again, it was down to royal patronage. Queen Victoria, a granddaughter of Queen Charlotte, was a great dog lover, with a keen interest in new breeds. On a royal visit to Florence, Italy, she came across the Pomeranian and was so taken by the breed that she brought several back to the UK.

Among the imported Poms was a red sable called

Marco. He weighed just 12lb (5.4kg), and when he was first exhibited, he created a flurry of interest. Breeders were intent on producing small-size Poms, and Queen Victoria maintained her interest, importing small Pomeranians of different colors from Europe. Among her show dogs were Gina, a white dog with lemon tinges, weighing 7.5lb (3.4kg), Lenda, a buff colored dog with a white blaze on her face, and Fluffy, the result of a Marco-Lenda mating, who was also buff colored.

In these early days, there were two size categories: over 8lb (3.6kg) and under 8lb. But such was the enthusiasm for small Poms that the entries for the larger size dwindled, and in 1894 there was a single category for dogs weighing below 7lb.

The Pom in the USA

The first record of a Pomeranian being shown in the USA is in 1894 when Sheffield Lad, owned by Mr Toon from Sheffield in the UK, took second place in the Westminster Kennel Club Show. He was entered in the miscellaneous class and was beaten by a Maltese Terrier.

In 1888, a Pomeranian, called Dick, was registered with the American Kennel Club, and by 1899, at the American Pet Dog Thanksgiving Show, there were nine classes scheduled for Pomeranians, and there were at least 18 Poms present. At this time, most of the imports came from the UK, and the most common colors were blue, black, white and brown.

It was in 1900 that the new breed received official recognition, and the American Pomeranian Club was formed. In 1911, the club held its first specialty show in New York and this has become an annual fixture.

Great survivor

When the Titanic sank in 1912, over 1500 people lost their lives – but one Pomeranian survived by escaping on to a lifeboat.

Soaring popularity

In the early years of the 20th century, the Pomeranian soared in popularity on both sides of the Atlantic, as the breed was discovered to be an outstanding companion as well as being a glamorous show dog.

Color breeding became the craze and more and more colors, markings and patterns were added. These included brindle, raccoon sable, dove, smoke blue, chocolate, grey sable, and wolf color. In the USA, there were even records of blue mottled Pomeranians.

Following the Second World War, it was the Pekingese and the Yorkshire Terrier that found favour, and the Pom was ousted in the popularity stakes.

Today it has made something of a comeback, particularly in the USA, where it is consistently ranked in the top 15 most popular breeds.

It was not long before breeders started to develop new colors for the breed.

What should a Pomeranian look like?

The Pomeranian looks like no other breed – a spitz dog in miniature – a dainty, compact companion dog, with all the spirit of his larger relatives. So what makes the Pom so special?

Breeders have been producing Pomeranians as we know them, for over a hundred years, retaining the appearance and characteristics that are so highly valued in the show ring and by pet owners. To achieve this, they are guided by a Breed Standard, which is a written blueprint describing what the perfect specimen should look like.

Of course, there is no such thing as a 'perfect' dog, but breeders aspire to produce dogs that conform as closely as possible to the picture in words presented

in the Breed Standard. In the show ring, judges use the Breed Standard to assess the dogs that come before them, and it is the dog that, in their opinion, comes closest to the ideal, that will win top honours.

This has significance beyond the sport of showing for it is the dogs that win in the ring that will be used for breeding. The winners of today are therefore responsible for passing on their genes to future generations and preserving the breed in its best form.

There are some differences in the wording of the Breed Standard depending on national Kennel Clubs; the American Standard is certainly more descriptive than the English version. It is also interesting to note that more colors and patterns are allowed in American dogs.

General appearance

The Pomeranian is a compact, short-backed dog of Nordic descent. He is a sturdy and well-constructed, yet still appears dainty. He is alert in character and shows great intelligence in expression. The American Breed Standard gives a colorful description of the Pom when he is moving, stating: "The Pomeranian is cocky, commanding and animated as he gaits".

Temperament

The Pom is described as an extrovert; he is vivacious
and lively, which makes him an ideal companion dog.
He not only has an intelligent expression, he is very
intelligent – and he thrives on mental stimulation.

*The Pomeranian is
unique in being sturdy
in build, yet still
appearing to be dainty.*

Head

The head is in balance with the body, and is fox-like in outline. The skull is slightly flat, and is large in relation to the muzzle on a ratio of two-thirds to one-third. The muzzle is fine with no trace of lippiness. The pigment of the nose varies depending on coat color; it is black in white, orange and shaded sable dogs, brown in chocolate tipped sables, and self-colored in other colors. It must never be part-colored or flesh-colored.

Eyes

Dark, bright and sparkling, the eyes hold the key to the Pomeranian's lively, intelligent expression. They are medium-sized and should not be set too wide apart. In white, orange, shaded sable and cream dogs, the eye-rims are black. The American Breed Standard disqualifies Poms that have light blue, blue marbled or blue flecked eyes.

Ears

The Pom's small ears are carried perfectly erect. They should not be too wide apart, or set too low down.

Mouth

The jaws are strong and the teeth should meet in a scissor bite, meaning the teeth on the upper jaw should closely overlap the teeth on the lower jaw.

Neck

The neck is relatively short and is set well into the shoulders. However, there must be sufficient length to allow the head to be carried proudly.

Forequarters

The shoulders are clean and well laid back. The elbows are close to the body and the front legs should be fine-boned and perfectly straight. They are medium length in proportion to the size of the dog.

Body

The back is level and short; the body is compact and well ribbed. The chest is fairly deep, but it should not be too wide.

Hindquarters

The rear angulation should be in balance with the forequarters. The legs, which are fine-boned, should not be wide behind, and the hocks should not turn inwards (cow-hocks).

Feet

The Pomeranian has small, neat, cat-like feet, which should be well arched and compact. They should not turn inwards or outwards.

Tail

The high-set tail, turned over the back, is a breed characteristic; a low-set tail is considered a major fault in the American Breed Standard. The tail should be carried flat and straight and it should be heavily plumed, with long, harsh, spreading hair.

Gait/movement

The Kennel Club Standard in the UK confines itself to a very brief description –" free moving, brisk and buoyant".

In contrast, the American Standard gives a far more detailed description. It states that the Pom should have good reach in the forequarters and strong drive from the rear, showing a gait that is smooth, free, balanced and brisk.

The head should remain high and proud while the dog is moving, and the overall outline should be maintained.

Coat

The Pomeranian has two coats; a soft, dense, fluffy undercoat and a long, straight topcoat, which is harsh in texture. The coat is abundant around the neck, shoulders and chest, forming a ruff (frill). The forequarters are well feathered and the thighs and hindlegs are feathered as far as the hocks. A soft, flat or open coat is considered a major fault in the American Breed Standard.

Color

One of the great delights on the breed is that it comes in all colors – but there are different stipulations in British and American Standards.

In America, all colors, patterns and variations are judged on an equal basis, although in Open classes at Specialty shows, classes may be divided by coat color as follows:

- Red

- Orange

- Cream and sable

- Black

- Brown and blue

- Any color allowed.

Facing page: A Pom can be any of the permitted colors with tan markings.

The requirements for color and markings are:

- Any solid color – white on the chest feet or legs is a major fault (except on white dogs).

- Any solid color with lighter or darker shading of that color.

- Any color with sable or black shading

- Parti-color – white with evenly distributed patches of solid color, and a white blaze on the head.

- Piebald – white with patches of color on the head, body and base of the tail.

- Extreme piebald – white with patches of color on the head and the base of the tail.

- Irish – color on the head and body, with white legs, chest and collar.

- Tan points – any color with clearly defined tan markings over each eye, on the muzzle, throat and forechest, on the legs and feet and the underside of the tail.

- Brindle – dark cross stripes on any solid color or allowed pattern.

In the British Breed Standard, whole colors are always preferred to the other patterns.

Size

The American Breed Standard allows for a weight range of 3-7lbs (1.3-3.1kg), but the ideal for show dogs is 4-5lb (1.8-2.2kg)

In the UK, males are slightly smaller than females, which is unusual in the dog world as it is usually the other way round. However, size needs to be taken into consideration in breeding as females may have whelping problems if they are too petite. The preferred weight for males is given as 4-4.5lb (1.8-2kg) compared to the female weight of 4.5-5.5lb (2-2.5kg).

Summing up

Despite the differences in relation to size and color, the Breed Standards agree on the major points of conformation, coat type, temperament and movement. Most importantly, breeders are striving to produce typical, healthy dogs, without exaggeration, who truly live up their reputation as outstanding companion dogs.

What do you want from your Pom?

Pomeranians are irresistible. Beautiful to look at, sturdy for their size, and highly intelligent – this is a Toy dog that will suit a wide variety of lifestyles. But before you take the plunge into Pom ownership, weigh up the pros and cons so you can be 100 per cent confident that this is the breed for you.

Companionship

The Pomeranian is the most loving and affectionate of dogs, and he often develops a fierce loyalty towards his family. If you want a dog to be with you, enjoying your company and joining in all activities, the Pom is the breed for you. Conversely, if you are committed to spending time away from home every day, this breed is not a good choice.

If you have children, are you considering a Pomeranian as a suitable playmate? If so, take care. The Pom is an extrovert, fun-loving dog, but he will not tolerate rough handling. If you have children under five, you should consider getting a more robust breed.

There are dog lovers who are getting on in years, or who may not be as mobile as they once were, who want a dog but are worried about fulfilling their exercise needs. In this situation, a Pom may well be the answer. This is a dog who will be perfectly happy pottering around in the garden or going for short walks.

Show dog

Do you have ambitions to exhibit your Pomeranian the show ring? This is a specialist sport, which often becomes highly addictive, but you do need the right dog to start with.

If you plan to show your Pom, you need to track down a show quality puppy, and train him so he will perform in the show ring, and accept the detailed 'hands on' examination that he will be subjected to when he is being judged.

You also need to accept that not every puppy with show potential develops into a top-quality specimen, and so you must be prepared to love your Pom and give him a home for life, even if he doesn't make the grade.

What does your Pom want from you?

A dog cannot speak for himself, so we need to view the world from a canine perspective and work out what a Pomeranian needs in order to live a happy, contented and fulfilling life.

Time and commitment

First of all, a Pom needs a commitment that you will care for him for the duration of his life – guiding him through his puppyhood, enjoying his adulthood, and being there for him in his later years. If all potential owners were prepared to make this pledge, there would be scarcely any dogs in rescue.

The Pomeranian excels as a companion dog, which means he thrives on being with his people. If you cannot give your

Pom the time and commitment he deserves, you would be strongly advised to delay owning a dog until your circumstances change.

Practical matters

As already highlighted, the Pomeranian is a breed that will suit many different lifestyles. He does not require the exercise that is so important for larger breeds, but when mature, he does have a massive coat. This needs intensive care, otherwise it will mat and tangle, causing serious discomfort to your Pom. You can enlist the help of a professional groomer, but, obviously, you will need to budget for this.

Mental stimulation

Although your Pom does not need to go hiking across the hills, he is a clever dog and he needs to use his brain. A bored dog quickly becomes destructive, or in the case of a Pom, he made decide to spend his time barking at every sound he hears. He is not being 'naughty' as we understand it; he is simply finding an occupation to fill the empty hours.

As a Pom owner, you must be responsible for providing mental stimulation; this can be in the form of training exercises, teaching tricks, trips out in the car, or going for short walks in different places so your Pom has the chance to explore and investigate new scents.

You also need to provide a sense of leadership so your Pom knows you are the decision-maker in the family. If he is left to his own devices, this highly intelligent little dog will run rings round you.

The clever Pom needs variety and interest in his life.

Extra
considerations

Now you have decided that a Pomeranian is the dog of your dreams, you can narrow your choice so you know exactly what you are looking for.

Male or female?

There are some Pom owners who swear that females are more loyal and affectionate than males – others say the opposite – so it all comes down to personal preference.

You may find a female, which is slightly bigger and heavier than the male, is harder to come by, or you may have to go on a waiting list. This is because Pomeranian litters are small, and the breeder often wants to keep a female for their own breeding program.

If you opt for a female, you will need to cope with her seasonal cycle, which will start at any time from six months, with seasons occurring twice yearly thereafter. During the three-week period of a season, you will need to keep your bitch away from entire males (males that have not been neutered) to eliminate the risk of an unwanted pregnancy.

Many pet owners opt for neutering, which puts an end to the seasons, and also and has many attendant health benefits. The operation, known as spaying, is usually carried out at some point after the first season. The best plan is to ask your vet for advice.

An entire male may not cause many problems, although some do have a stronger tendency to mark, which could include the house. However, training will usually put a stop to this. An entire male will also be on the lookout for bitches in season, and this may lead to difficulties, depending on your circumstances.

Neutering (castrating) a male is a relatively simple operation, and there are associated health benefits. Again, you should seek advice from your vet.

Color

There are so many colors to choose from in Pomeranians, you are spoilt for choice. However, finding a particular color may pose a problem as some are quite rare, particularly in the UK where there is a much smaller gene pool and far fewer colors are readily available.

The most popular colors are orange, cream and shaded varieties, In the UK, whole colors are preferred in the show ring, so breeders focus on producing these.

In the USA all colors are of equal merit, and so there

is a far wider selection of patterns and markings; parti-colors are always in demand.

More than one?

Pomeranians are sociable dogs and certainly enjoy each other's company. But you would be wise to guard against the temptation of getting two puppies of similar ages, or even two from the same litter.

Unfortunately there are some unscrupulous breeders who encourage people to do this, but they are thinking purely in terms of profit, and not considering the welfare of the puppies.

Looking after one puppy is hard work, but taking on two pups at the same time is more than double the workload. House training is a nightmare as, often, you don't even know which puppy is making mistakes, and training is impossible unless you separate the two puppies and give them one-on-one attention.

The puppies will never be bored as they have each other to play with. However, the likelihood is that they will form a close bond, and you will come a poor second.

If you do decide to add to your Pomeranian population, wait at least 18 months so your first dog is fully trained and settled before taking on a puppy.

Facing page: Two pups of the same age will be more than double the workload.

An older dog

You may decide to miss out on the puppy phase and take on an older dog instead. Such a dog may be harder to track down, but sometimes a breeder may have a youngster that is not suitable for showing, but is perfect for a family pet. In some cases, a breeder may rehome a female when her breeding career is at an end so she will enjoy the benefits of getting more individual attention.

There are advantages to taking on an older dog, as you know exactly what you are getting. But the upheaval of changing homes can be quite upsetting, so you will need to have plenty of patience during the settling in period.

Rehoming a rescued dog

We are fortunate that the number of Poms that end up in rescue is relatively small, and this is often through no fault of the dog. The reasons are various, ranging from illness or death of the original owner to family breakdown, changing jobs, or even the arrival of a new baby.

It is unlikely that you will find a Pomeranian in an all-breed rescue centre, but the specialist breed clubs run rescue schemes, and this will be your best option if you decide to go down this route.

Try to find out as much as you can about the dog's history so you know exactly what you are taking on. You need to be realistic about what you are capable of achieving so you can be sure you can give the dog in question a permanent home.

Again, you need to give a rescued Pom plenty of time and patience as he settles into his new home, but if all goes well, you will have the reward of knowing that you have given your dog a second chance.

Sourcing a puppy

If you plan to start with a puppy, make a shortlist of suitable breeders so you can go and see different stock, and check that you are happy with the breeder and set-up. The more you talk with people about their dogs, the more you will learn and the easier it will be to make an informed decision.

The internet is an excellent resource, but when it comes to finding a puppy, use it with care:

Do go to the website of your national Kennel Club.

Both the American Kennel Club (AKC) and the Kennel Club (KC) have excellent websites that will give you information about Pomeranians, and what to look for when choosing a puppy. You will also find contact details for specialist breed clubs.

Both sites have lists of puppies available, and you can look out for breeders of merit (AKC) and assured breeders (KC) which indicates that they have followed a code of conduct.

Do find details of specialist breed clubs.

On breed club websites you will find information about the breed and Pomeranian breeders in your area. Some websites also have a list of breeders that have puppies available. The advantage of going through a breed club is that there will be a code of ethics that breeders must adhere to. This will give you some guarantees regarding stock and health checks.

Do not look at websites simply listing puppies for sale.

There are legitimate Pomeranian breeders with their own websites, and they may, occasionally, advertise a litter, although in most cases reputable breeders have waiting lists for their puppies. The danger comes from unscrupulous breeders that produce puppies purely for profit, with no thought for the health of the dogs they breed from and no care given to rearing the litter. Photos of puppies are hard to resist, but never make a decision based purely on an advertisement. You need to find out who the breeder is, and have the opportunity to visit their premises and inspect the litter before making a decision.

Questions, questions, questions

When you find a breeder with puppies available, you will have lots of questions to ask. These should include the following:

- Where have the puppies been reared? Hopefully, they will be in a home environment, which gives them the best possible start in life.

- How many are in the litter?

- What is the split of males and females?

- How many have already been spoken for?

- What colors are available?

- Can I see the mother with her puppies?

- What age are the puppies?

- When will they be ready to go to their new homes?

Bear in mind puppies need to be with their mother and siblings until they are eight weeks of age, otherwise they miss out on vital learning and communication skills which will have a detrimental effect on them for the rest of their lives. Most breeders of Toy dogs prefer to keep the puppies a little longer – until they are 10-12 weeks of age – when they are bigger and ready to face the world.

You should also be prepared to answer a number

of searching questions so the breeder can check if you are suitable as a potential owner of one of their precious puppies.

You will be asked some or all of the following questions:

- What is your home set up?

- Do you have children/grandchildren?

- What are their ages?

- Is there somebody at home most of the time?

- What is your previous experience with dogs?

- Do you have plans to show your Pomeranian?

The breeder is not being intrusive; they need to understand the environment you will be able to provide for your new dog in order to make the right match. Do not object to this, as the breeder is doing it for both the dog's benefit and also for your own.

Be very wary of a breeder who does not ask you questions. He or she may be more interested in making money out of the puppies rather than ensuring that they go to good homes. They may also have taken other short cuts which may prove disastrous, and very expensive, in terms of vet bills or plain heartache.

Health issues

The Pomeranian suffers from few hereditary problems but, although there are no health tests required for breeding stock at the moment, you would be advised to talk to the breeder about the health status of their dogs and find out if there are any issues of concern.

Waiting game

Pomeranian litters tend to be small; they are mostly two to three puppies, four if you are lucky, but singletons are not uncommon. For this reason you may have to put your name on a waiting list, particularly if you want a show quality puppy, or you want one of the rarer colors. This may seem frustrating, but when you bear in mind that a Pomeranian will be in your life for the next 12 years or so, it is worth being patient and waiting for the puppy of your dreams.

Essentially, you are looking for a fit, clean, happy, healthy puppy that is typical of the breed and is likely to live to a ripe old age. In order to avoid unnecessary heartache it is best to be patient and find the right puppy for you, from the correct source.

Puppy watching

Puppies are irresistible, and when you go to see a litter of Pomeranian pups, you will be well and truly smitten. But this is a time when you must not let your heart rule your head. You must be 100 per cent confident that the breeding stock is healthy, and the puppies have been reared with love and care, before making a commitment to buy.

Viewing a litter

It is a good idea to have mental checklist of what to discover when you visit a breeder. Look out for the following:

- A clean, hygienic environment.

- Puppies who are out-going and friendly, and eager to meet you.

- A sweet-natured mother who is ready to show off her babies.

- Puppies that are well covered, but not pot-bellied, which could be an indication of worms.

- Bright eyes, with no sign of soreness or discharge.

- Clean ears that smell fresh.

- No discharge from the nose.

- Clean rear ends – matting could indicate upset tummies.

- Lively pups who are keen to play.

- It is important that you see the mother with her puppies as this will give you a good idea of the temperament they are likely to inherit. It is also helpful if you can see other close relatives so you can see the type of Pomeranian the breeder produces.

In most cases, you will not be able to see the father (sire) as most breeders will travel some distance to find a stud dog that is not too close to their own bloodlines and complements their bitch. However, you should be able to see photos of him and be given the chance to examine his pedigree and show record.

Companion puppy

If you are looking for a Pomeranian as a companion, you should be guided by the breeder who will have spent hours and hours puppy watching, and will know each of the pups as individuals.

The breeder may well be keeping a puppy and, as Pom litters tend to be small, there may only be a couple of pups to choose from. The breeder will take into account your family set up and lifestyle and will help to pick the most suitable puppy.

Color

By the time a Pomeranian puppy is six weeks of age, the breeder should have a good idea of what color he will be when he matures. The true color usually comes through first at the base of the ear. However, it is not unknown for the coat to change at a later stage; for example, an orange sable puppy may lose his sable color as the adult coat comes through.

Show puppy

If you are picking a puppy with the hope of showing him, try to go with someone who has expert knowledge and will give their objective opinion. The breeder will also be there to help as they will want to ensure that only the best of their stock is exhibited in the show ring.

Look out for a puppy with the following attributes:

- A well-balanced body: a Pomeranian in miniature.

- The correct scissor bite (see page 34), although this cannot be guaranteed to remain correct until the adult teeth come through.

- A tail that is set on high and lies straight over the back.

- An extrovert, out-going temperament.

A Pom-friendly home

It may seem an age before your Pomeranian puppy is ready to leave the breeder and move to his new home. But you can fill time by getting your home ready, and buying the equipment you will need. These preparations apply to a new puppy but, in reality, they are the means of creating an environment that is safe and secure for your Pom throughout his life.

In the home

The Pomeranian is lively and inquisitive, which means he can get into all sorts of trouble unless you have carried out essential safety checks.

Trailing electric cables are a major hazard and these will need to be secured out of reach. You will need to make sure all cupboards are secure, particularly in the kitchen where you may store cleaning materials which could be toxic to dogs. Household plants can also be poisonous, so these will need to relocated, along with breakable ornaments.

You may decide to exclude your puppy from some rooms, and even though he will be too small to go upstairs to begin with, it may be easier to make upstairs off-limits right from the start. The best way of doing this is to use a baby gate, making sure your puppy cannot squeeze through, which could result in injury.

Before your puppy comes home, hold a family conference to decide on the house rules. For example, is your Pom going to be allowed on the sofa or not? This is a personal choice, but whatever you decide, you, and everyone else in the family, must be consistent, otherwise your puppy will become very confused.

In the garden

A Pomeranian puppy is so tiny that even an average-sized garden will seem enormous. In the first few weeks, it may be advisable to allow him access to a small part of it by rigging up some temporary fencing. Regardless of whether you decide to do this or not, you will need to check all boundary fencing, just in case your Pom finds an escape route. Gates leading from the garden should have secure fastenings.

If you are a keen gardener, you may want to protect your prized plants from unwanted attention. There are a number of flowers and shrubs that are toxic to dogs, so check this out on the Internet (you will find a list at dogbooksonline.co.uk) or by seeking advice from your local garden centre. You will also need to designate a toileting area. This will assist the house training process, and it will also make cleaning up easier. For information on house-training, see page 90.

Buying equipment

There are some essential items of equipment you will need for your Pomeranian. If you choose wisely, much of it will last for many years to come.

Indoor crate

Rearing a puppy is so much easier if you invest in an indoor crate. It provides a safe haven for your puppy at night, when you have to go out during the day, and at other times when you cannot supervise him. A puppy does need a base where he feels safe and secure, and where he can rest undisturbed. An indoor crate provides the perfect den, and many adults continue to use them throughout their lives.

You will also need to consider where you are going to locate the crate. The kitchen is usually the most suitable place as this is the hub of the household and the room in which most members of the family will spend most of their time. Try to find a snug corner where the puppy can rest when he wants to, but where he can also see what is going on around him, and still be with the family.

Beds and bedding

The crate will need to be lined with bedding and the best type to buy is synthetic fleece. This is warm and cosy, and, as moisture soaks through it, your puppy will not have a wet bed when he is tiny and is still unable to go through the night without relieving himself. This type of bedding is machine washable and easy to dry; buy two pieces, so you have one to use while the other piece is in the wash.

If you have purchased a crate, you may not feel the need to buy an extra bed, although many Poms like to have an extra bed in the family room so they feel part of household activities. There is an amazing array of dog-beds to chose from – duvets, bean bags, cushions, baskets, igloos, mini-four posters – so you can take your pick!

Collar and leash

You may think that it is not worth buying a collar for the first few weeks, but the sooner your pup gets used to it, the better. All you need is a lightweight puppy collar; you can buy something more exotic when your Pom is fully grown.

A nylon leash is suitable for early training, but make sure the fastening is secure. Again, you can invest in a more expensive leash at a later date – there are lots of attractive collar and leash sets to choose from.

ID

Your Pomeranian needs to wear some form of ID when he is out in public places. This can be in form of a disc, engraved with your contact details, that can be attached to the collar. When your Pom is older, you can buy an embroidered collar with your contact details, which eliminates the danger of the disc becoming detached from the collar.

You may also wish to consider a permanent form of ID. More and more breeders are microchipping puppies before they go to their new homes. A microchip is the size of a grain of rice. It is 'injected' under the skin, usually between the shoulder blades with a special needle. It has some tiny barbs on it, which dig into the tissue around where it lies, so it does not migrate from that spot.

Each chip has its own unique identification number which can only be read by a special scanner. That ID number is then registered on a national database with your name and details, so that if ever your dog is lost, he can be taken to any vet or rescue centre where he is scanned and then you are contacted.

If your puppy has not been microchipped, you can ask your vet to do it, maybe when he goes for his vaccinations.

Bowls

Your Pom will need two bowls; one for food, and one for fresh drinking water, which should always be readily available. A stainless steel bowl is a good choice for a food bowl as it is tough and hygienic. Plastic bowls may be chewed, and there is a danger that bacteria can collect in the small cracks that may appear.

You can opt for a second stainless steel bowl for drinking water, or you may prefer a heavier ceramic bowl which will not be knocked over so easily.

Food

The breeder will let you know what your puppy is eating and should provide a full diet sheet to guide you through the first six months of your puppy's feeding regime – how much they are eating per meal, how many meals per day, when to increase the amounts given per meal and when to reduce the meals per day.

The breeder may provide you with some food when you collect your puppy, but it is worth making enquiries in advance about the availability of the brand that is recommended.

Grooming equipment

Your Pomeranian will have an abundant coat when he is fully mature so it is important that he gets used to being groomed from an early age. The full grooming kit you will need for an adult includes the following:

- A good-quality bristle brush

- A double-ended comb with fine teeth at one end, and wide teeth at the other

- Guillotine nail clippers

- Toothbrush (a finger brush is easiest to use) and specially-manufactured dog toothpaste

- Scissors to trim the coat.

- Cotton pads for cleaning the eyes and ears

- Mild dog shampoo.

Toys

The Pomeranian loves to play, and this trait will stay with him for most of his life. Any type of toy is fine – squeaky toys, tug toys, rubber kongs, which can be filled with food, and soft toys. Your guiding principle when choosing a toy must be whether it is suitably robust. A Pom may have small teeth, but he can still do a fair amount of damage. When he is teething, from around four months of age, a puppy will have a great urge to chew, and nothing will be safe.

Finding a vet

Before your puppy arrives home, you should register with a vet. Visit vets in your local area, and speak to other pet owners you might know, to see who they recommend. You need to find a vet with whom you can build up a good rapport, and have complete faith in.

When you contact a veterinary practice, find out the following:

- Does the surgery run an appointment system?

- What are the arrangements for emergency, out of hours cover?

- Do any of the vets in the practice have experience treating Pomeranians?

- What facilities are available at the practice?

If you are satisfied with what your find, and the staff appear helpful and friendly, book an appointment so your puppy can have a health check a couple of days after you collect him.

Settling in

When you first arrive home with your puppy, be careful not to overwhelm him. You and your family are hugely excited, but the puppy is in a completely strange environment with new sounds, smells and sights, which is a daunting experience, even for the most confident of pups.

Some puppies want to play straightaway and quickly make friends; others need a little longer. Keep a close check on your Pom's body language and reactions so you can proceed at a pace he is comfortable with.

First, let him explore the garden. He will probably need to relieve himself after the journey home, so take him to the allocated toileting area and, when he performs, give him plenty of praise.

When you take your puppy indoors, let him investigate again. Show him where you have located his crate, and encourage him to go in by throwing in a treat. Let him have a sniff, and let him come out when he wants

to. Later on, when he is tired, you can put him in the crate while you stay in the room, so that he learns to settle and doesn't think he is being abandoned.

It is a good idea if you feed your puppy in his crate, at least to begin with, as it helps to build up a positive association. It will not take long before your Pomeranian sees his crate as his own special place. Some owners place a blanket over the crate, covering the back and sides, so that it is even more cosy and den-like.

Meeting the family

Resist the temptation of inviting friends and neighbors to come and meet the new arrival; your puppy needs to focus on getting to know his new family for the first few days. Try not to swamp your Pom with too much attention; give him a chance to explore and find his feet. There will be plenty of time for cuddles later on!

If you have children, you need to keep everything as calm as possible so your puppy does not get alarmed by too much noise.

The best plan is to get the children to sit on the floor and give them all a treat. Each child can then call the puppy, stroke him, and offer a treat. In this way the puppy is making the decisions rather than being forced into interactions he may find stressful.

Facing page: If early interactions are supervized, a Pom will respect all members of his human family.

It is a good idea to impose a rule, right from the start, that children are not allowed to pick up or carry the puppy. They can cuddle him when they are sitting on the floor. This may sound a little severe, but a wriggly puppy can be dropped in an instant, sometimes with disastrous consequences

Involve all family members with the day-to-day care of your puppy; this will enable the bond to develop with the whole family as opposed to just one person. Encourage the children to train and reward the puppy, teaching him to follow their commands without question.

The animal family

Pomeranians are rarely a problem when it comes to living with other dogs. However, it is important to supervise early interactions so relations with the resident dog get off on a good footing.

Your adult dog may be allowed to meet the puppy at the home of the breeder, which is ideal as the older dog will not feel threatened if he is away from his own home. But if this is not possible, allow your dog to smell the puppy's bedding (the bedding supplied by the breeder is fine) before they actually meet so he familiarizes himself with the puppy's scent.

The garden is the best place for introducing the puppy, as the adult will regard it as neutral territory. He will probably take a great interest in the puppy and sniff him all over. Most puppies are naturally submissive in this situation, and your pup may lick the other dog's mouth or roll over on to his back. Try not to interfere as this is the natural way that dogs get to know each other.

You will only need to intervene if the older dog is too boisterous, and alarms the puppy. In this case, it is a good idea to put the adult on his leash so you have some measure of control.

It rarely takes long for an adult to accept a puppy, particularly if you make a big fuss of the older dog so that he still feels special. However, do not take any risks and supervise all interactions for the first few weeks. If you do need to leave the dogs alone, always make sure your puppy is safe in his crate.

Meeting a cat should be supervised in a similar way, but do not allow your puppy to be rough. The cat may retaliate using its sharp claws, which could inflict an injury. A Pom can be very excitable and may try running up and barking at the cat. Make sure you stop this straightaway before bad habits develop.

Generally, the Pom-feline relationship should not cause any serious problems. Indeed, many Poms and cats end up the best of friends.

Feeding

The breeder will generally provide enough food for the first few days so the puppy does not have to cope with a change in diet – and possible digestive upset – along with all the stress of moving home.

Some puppies eat up from the first meal onwards, others are more concerned by their new surroundings and are too distracted to bother. Do not worry unduly if your puppy seems disinterested in his food for the first day or so. Give him 10 minutes to eat what he wants and then remove the leftovers and start afresh at the next meal.

Do not make the mistake of trying to tempt his appetite with tasty treats or you will end up with a faddy feeder. This is a mistake made by all too many Pom owners, and a scenario can develop where the dog holds out, refusing to eat his food, in the hope that something better will be offered.

Below: Make sure your puppy is not too pushy when he first meets the family cat.

Obviously if you have any concerns about your puppy in the first few days, seek advice from your vet.

The first night

Your puppy will have spent the first weeks of his life with his mother or curled up with his siblings. He is then taken from everything he knows as familiar, lavished with attention by his new family – and then comes bed time when he is left all alone. It is little wonder that he feels abandoned.

The best plan is to establish a night-time routine, and then stick to it so that your puppy knows what is expected of him. Take your puppy out into the garden to relieve himself, and then settle him in his crate. Some people leave a low light on for the puppy at night for the first week, others have tried a radio as company or a ticking clock. A covered hot-water bottle, filled with warm water, can also be a comfort. Like people, puppies are all individuals and what works for one does not necessarily work for another, so it is a matter of trial and error.

Be very positive when you leave your puppy on his own; do not linger, or keep returning – this will make the situation more difficult. It is inevitable that he will protest to begin with. But, if you stick to your routine, he will accept that he gets left at night and you always return in the morning.

Rescued dogs

Settling an older, rescued dog in the home is very similar to a puppy in as much as you will need to make the same preparations regarding his homecoming. As with a puppy, an older dog will need you to be consistent, so start as you mean to go on.

There is often an initial honeymoon period when you bring a rescued dog home. He will be on his best behavior for the first few weeks, then his true nature will show, so be prepared for subtle changes in his behavior. It may be advisable to register with a reputable training club, so you can seek advice on any training or behavioral issues at an early stage.

Above all, remember that a rescued dog ceases to be a rescued dog the moment he enters his forever home and should be treated like any other family pet.

House training

This is an aspect of training that most first-time puppy owners dread, but it should not be a problem as along as you are prepared to put in the time and effort.

When you were preparing for your puppy's homecoming, you will have allocated a toileting area in your garden. You need to take your puppy to this area every time he needs to relieve himself so he builds up an association and knows why you have brought him out to the garden.

Establish a routine and make sure you take your puppy out at the following times:

- First thing in the morning
- After mealtimes
- On waking from a sleep
- Following a play session

- Last thing at night.

A puppy should be taken out to relieve himself every two hours as an absolute minimum. If you can manage an hourly trip, so much the better. The more your puppy gets it 'right', the quicker he will learn to be clean in the house.

It helps if you use a verbal cue, such as "Busy", when your pup is performing and, in time, this will trigger the desired response.

Do not be tempted to put your puppy out on the doorstep in the hope that he will toilet on his own. Most pups simply sit there, waiting to get back inside the house! No matter how bad the weather is, accompany your puppy and give him lots of praise when he performs correctly.

Do not rush back inside as soon as he has finished. Your puppy might start to delay in the hope of prolonging his time outside with you. Praise him, have a quick game – and then you can both return indoors.

When accidents happen

No matter how vigilant you are, there are bound to be accidents. If you witness the accident, take your puppy outside immediately, and give him lots of praise if he finishes his business out there.

If you are not there when he has an accident, do not scold him when you discover what has happened. He will not remember what he has done and will not understand why you are cross with him. Simply clean it up and resolve to be more vigilant next time.

It will not take long before your puppy understands that he must be clean in the house.

Make sure you use a deodorizer, available in pet stores, when you clean up, otherwise your pup will be drawn to the smell and may be tempted to use the same spot again.

Choosing
a diet

There are so many different types of
dog food to choose from, it can be
bewildering for the first-time owner.
Your Pomeranian may be a tiny Toy dog,
but he still needs a high-quality, well-
balanced diet.

When choosing a diet, there are basically three
categories to choose from:

Complete

This is probably the most popular diet as it is easy
to feed and is specially formulated with all the
nutrients your dog needs. This means that you
should not add any supplements or you may upset
the nutritional balance.

Most complete diets come in different life stages:
puppy, adult maintenance and senior, so this means
that your Pom is getting what he needs when he is

growing, during adulthood, and as he becomes older. You can even get prescription diets for dogs with particular health issues.

There are many different brands to choose from so it is advisable to seek advice from your puppy's breeder, who will have lengthy experience of feeding Poms.

Canned/pouches

This type of food is usually fed with hard biscuit, and most Poms find it very appetizing. However, the ingredients – and the nutritional value – do vary significantly between the different brands so you will need to check the label. This type of food often has a high moisture content, so you need to be sure your Pom is getting all the nutrition he needs.

Homemade

There are some owners who like to prepare meals especially for their dogs. If this is a route you want to go down, you will need to find out the exact ratio of fats, carbohydrates, proteins, minerals and vitamins that are needed, as it is important to ensure your dog's food contains the correct nutritional balance.

The Barf (Biologically Appropriate Raw Food) diet is another, more natural approach to feeding. Dogs are fed a diet mimicking what they would have eaten in the wild, consisting of raw chicken meat, bone,

Facing page: Complete diets are specially manufactured to suit your dog's age and lifestyle.

muscle, fat, and vegetable matter. Some owners worry that Toy breeds cannot cope with this diet, but there is evidence that they do well on it, particularly as many small dogs are prone to dental problems. The best plan is to seek advice from your vet.

Feeding regime

When your puppy arrives in his new home he will need four meals, evenly spaced throughout the day. You may decide to keep to the diet recommended by your puppy's breeder, and if your pup is thriving there is no need to change. However, if your puppy is not doing well on the food, or you have problems with supply, you will need to make a change.

When switching diets, it is very important to do it on a gradual basis, changing over from one food to the next, a little at a time, and spreading the transition over a week to 10 days. This will avoid the risk of digestive upset.

When your puppy is around 12 weeks, you can cut out one of his meals; he may well have started to leave some of his food indicating he is ready to do this. By six months, he can move on to two meals a day – a regime that will suit him for the rest of his life.

Bones and chews

Puppies love to chew, and many adults also enjoy gnawing on a bone. However, you need to be very careful with a Pomeranian as they have tiny jaws. Bones should always be hard and uncooked; rib bones and poultry bones must be avoided as they can splinter and cause major problems. Dental chews, and some of the manufactured rawhide chews, are safe, but they should only be given under supervision.

Another safe option is to give your Pom a hard dog biscuit, which he will gnaw and break up into smaller pieces. They are easy to consume.

Ideal weight

In order to help to keep your Pomeranian in good health it is necessary to monitor his weight. It is all too easy for the pounds to pile on, and this can result in serious health problems.

With a Pom, it can be difficult to see if he is gaining weight because of his abundant coat. Poms are also very clever at fixing you with an intent gaze, and pleading with you for a tiny morsel.

In order to keep a close check on your Pom's weight, get into the habit of weighing him every month and keep a record, so you can make adjustments if necessary.

If you are concerned that your Pom is putting on too much weight, consult your vet who will help you to plan a suitable diet.

Caring
for your
Pomeranian

The Pomeranian is a relatively high-maintenance breed but, if you establish a good regime of care management, it will simply become part of your weekly routine.

Grooming

The Pom's crowning glory is his coat, but it does need a fair amount of grooming to keep it in tip-top condition.

It is important to accustom your puppy to being groomed from an early age. It is beneficial to train your puppy to stand on a table for this procedure; he will learn that this is the place where he is groomed – and it will also save your back!

Start off by using a good-quality bristle brush and spend a few minutes every day grooming his coat. To begin with, your puppy will wriggle and may try to bite the brush, but just be firm and patent. As soon as he relaxes, and stops struggling, reward him with a treat. In time, he will start to enjoy his grooming sessions, and it will help to establish a bond between you and your dog. Many owners find grooming therapeutic, and there is no doubt that Poms love the special attention they receive.

As the adult coat comes through, the workload increases. You should reckon to give your Pomeranian a quick brush every day, and a thorough groom at least twice a week.

There is a special technique involved in brushing the coat:

- The leg, chest, tail, back and neck hair needs to be brushed upwards towards the head.

- The head hair is also brushed upwards.

- The hair on the undercarriage (tummy) is brushed downwards, towards the ground.

- The hair on the sides is brushed outwards so that it stands out at 90 degrees from the body.

The aim is to create a round, puffball shape.

The hair on the chest is brushed upwards.

Next, work through the coat with a comb.

A slicker brush should be used for mats and tangles.

When you are brushing, make sure you get through to the undercoat, to prevent mats forming. Once you have finished brushing, you need to go through the whole process again, this time using a comb. First use the wide-toothed end of the comb, and once you are sure the coat is tangle free, you can work through it again with the fine-toothed end of the comb.

Some parts of the coat are more prone to matting than others, such as behind the ears and below the chin. You may find it helpful to use a small slicker brush for these parts.

Trimming

This is not strictly necessary for pet owners, but a little careful scissoring will help to keep the coat neat and tidy as well as enhancing your Pom's appearance.

- The feathering on the front legs and hindquarters can get a little long and straggly, so this can be trimmed.

- You can neaten the shape of your Pom's ears by carefully trimming the hair that grows close to the edges.

- For hygiene purposes, trim the hair around the anus.

Facing page: When grooming and trimming, the aim is to create a round, puffball shape.

- The hair at the base of the tail can be trimmed to allow the tail to lie flat on the back.

- Hair growing between the pads should be trimmed, and the hair around the feet should also be trimmed to give a neat, cat-like appearance.

Bathing

If you bath a dog too often, it removes the natural oils in the coat, so it should only be done when necessary. Show dogs may be bathed more frequently, but even so, care is taken to bath a few days' in advance of the show, otherwise the coat loses its harsh texture, which is required according to the Breed Standard.

Make sure you use a shampoo specifically for dogs and resist the temptation of using a conditioner. It may make grooming easier but, again, it will destroy the natural texture of the coat by making it too soft.

Routine care

In addition to grooming, you will need to carry out some routine care.

Eyes

Check the eyes for signs of soreness or discharge. You can use a piece of cotton (cotton wool), a separate piece for each eye, and wipe away any debris.

Ears

The ears should be clean and free from odor. You can buy specially-manufactured ear wipes, or you can use a piece of cotton to clean them if necessary. Do not probe into the ear canal or you risk doing more harm than good.

Teeth

Dental disease is becoming more prevalent among dogs, so teeth cleaning should be seen as an essential part of your care regime. This applies most particularly to Toy dogs, who tend to have more problems with their teeth than other breeds. The build up of tartar on the teeth can result in tooth decay, gum infection and bad breath, and if it is allowed to accumulate, you may have no option but to get the teeth cleaned under anesthetic.

When your Pom is still a puppy accustom him to teeth cleaning so it becomes a matter of routine. Dog toothpaste comes in a variety of meaty flavours which your Pom will like, so you can start by putting some toothpaste on your finger and gently rubbing his teeth. You can then progress to using a finger brush or a toothbrush, whichever you find most convenient.

Remember to reward your Pom when he co-operates and then he will positively look forward to his teeth-cleaning sessions.

Nails

Nail trimming is a task dreaded by many owners – and many dogs – but, again, if you start early on, your Pom will get used to the procedure.

Pomeranians should have dark nails, and these are harder to trim than white nails as you cannot see the quick (the vein that runs through the nail) which will bleed if it is nicked. The best policy is to trim little and often so the nails don't grow too long, and you do not risk cutting too much and catching the quick.

If you are worried about trimming your Pom's nails, go to your vet so you can see it done properly. If you are still concerned, you can always use the services of a professional groomer.

Exercise

The Pomeranian is very adaptable when it comes to exercise, but this does not mean that he is content with the bare minimum.

Exercise gives a dog the opportunity to use his nose and investigate new sights and smells, so even if he does not go for miles, he will appreciate walks. A Pom is not built for strenuous exercise, so plan your walks with this in mind.

If, for any reason, your time is limited, it is useful if you can teach your Pom to retrieve a toy. He will expend a lot of energy playing this game and he will also enjoy the mental stimulation.

The older pom

We are fortunate the Pom has a good life expectancy, and you will not notice any significant changes in your Pom until he reaches double figures. Obviously all Poms are individuals and some will show signs of ageing earlier than others.

The older Pom will sleep more, and he may be reluctant to go for longer walks. You may find that he becomes more stressed in hot weather, so make sure his exercise is limited in these conditions. He may show signs of stiffness when he gets up from his bed, but these generally ease when he starts

moving. Some older Poms may have impaired vision, and some may become a little deaf.

If you treat your older Pom with kindness and consideration, he will enjoy his later years and suffer the minimum of discomfort. It is advisable to switch him over to a senior diet, which is more suited to his needs, and you may need to adjust the quantity, as he will not be burning up the calories as he did when he was younger and more energetic. Make sure his sleeping quarters are warm and free from draughts, and if he gets wet, make sure you dry him thoroughly.

Be aware of the
changing needs of your
Pom as he grows older.

Most important of all, be guided by your Pom. He will have good days when he feels up to going for a walk, and days when he would prefer to potter in the garden. If you have a younger dog at home, this may well stimulate your Pom but make sure he is not pestered, as he needs to rest undisturbed when he is tired.

Letting go

Inevitably there comes a time when your Pom is not enjoying a good quality of life, and you need to make the painful decision to let him go. We would all wish that our dogs died, painlessly, in their sleep but, unfortunately, this is rarely the case.

However, we can allow our dogs to die with dignity, and to suffer as a little as possible, and this should be our way of saying thank you for the wonderful companionship they have given us.

When you feel the time is drawing close, talk to your vet who will be able to make an objective assessment of your Pom's condition and will help you to make the right decision.

This is the hardest thing you will ever have to do as a dog owner, and it is only natural to grieve for your beloved Pom. But eventually, you will be able to look back on the happy memories of times spent together, and this will bring much comfort. You may, in time, feel that your life is not complete without a Pomeranian, and you feel ready to welcome a new puppy into your home.

Social skills

To live in the modern world, without fear and anxiety, a Pomeranian needs to receive an education in social skills so that he learns to cope with a wide variety of situations.

Early learning

The breeder will have started a program of socialization, getting the puppies used to all the sights and sounds of a busy household. You need to continue this when your pup arrives in his new home, making sure he is not worried by household equipment, such the vacuum cleaner, the washing machine, and that he gets used to unexpected noises from the radio and television.

It is important that you handle your puppy on a regular basis so he will accept grooming and other routine care, and will not be worried if he has to be examined by a vet.

To begin with, your puppy needs to get used to all the members of his new family, but then you should give him the opportunity to meet friends and other people that come to the house. A Pomeranian is a natural watchdog, and while a warning bark is acceptable, you do not want your Pom to continue barking at visitors.

Make sure you have some treats at the ready, and once your puppy has said his first 'hello', distract his attention by calling him to you and giving him a treat. You can also give the visitor a couple of treats, so that when your puppy approaches – and is not barking – he can be rewarded. This may take a bit of practice, but it is well worth persevering; the alternative is to invest in some earplugs!

If you do not have children, make sure your puppy has the chance to meet and play with other children, so he learns that people come in small sizes, too.

Allow your puppy to get used to new experiences at his own pace.

The outside world

When your puppy has completed his vaccinations, he is ready to venture into the outside world. Most Poms are reasonably bold, but for a small puppy there is a lot to take on board, so do not swamp him with too many new experiences when you first set out.

The best plan is to start in a quiet area with light traffic, and only progress to a busier place when your puppy is ready. There is so much to see and hear – people (maybe carrying bags or umbrellas), pushchairs, bicycles, cars, trucks, machinery – so give your puppy a chance to take it all in.

If he does appear worried, do not fall into the trap of sympathizing with him, or worse still, picking him up. This will only teach your pup that he had a good reason to be worried and, with luck, you will 'rescue' him if he feels scared.

Instead, give a little space so he does not have to confront whatever he is frightened of, and distract him with a few treats. Then encourage him to walk past, using a calm, no nonsense approach. Your pup will take the lead from you, and will realize there is nothing to fear.

Facing page: A well-socialized puppy will mature into a calm, confident adult.

Your pup also needs to continue his education in canine manners, started by his mother and by his littermates, as he needs to be able to greet all dogs calmly and confidently. If you have a friend who has a dog of sound temperament, this is an ideal beginning. As your puppy gets older and more established, you can widen his circle of canine acquaintances.

Training classes

A training class will give your Pom the opportunity to interact with other dogs, and he will also learn to focus on you in a different, distracting environment.

Before you go along with your puppy, it is worth attending a class as an observer to make sure you are happy with what goes on.

Find out the following:

- How much training experience do the instructors have?

- Are the classes divided into appropriate age categories?

- Do the instructors have experience training Toy dogs, and Poms in particular?

- Do they use positive, reward-based training methods?

If the training class is well run, it is certainly worth attending. Both you and your Pom will learn useful training exercises, it will increase his social skills, and you will have the chance to talk to lots of like-minded dog enthusiasts.

Training guidelines

We are fortunate that the Pom is a bright little dog and he is easy to teach, as long as you make his training sessions enjoyable.

You will be keen to get started, but in your rush to get his training underway, do not neglect the fundamentals that could make the difference between success and failure.

When you start training, try to observe the following guidelines:

- Choose an area that is free from distractions so your puppy will focus on you. You can progress to a more challenging environment as your pup progresses.

- Do not train your puppy just after he has eaten or when you have returned from exercise. He will either be too full, or too tired, to concentrate.

- Do not train if you are in a bad mood, or if you are short of time – these sessions always end in disaster!

- Make sure you have a reward your Pom values – tasty treats, such as cheese or cooked liver, or an extra special toy.

- If you are using treats, make sure they are bite-size, otherwise you will lose momentum when your pup stops to chew on his treat.

- Keep your verbal cues simple, and always use the same one for each exercise. For example, when you ask your puppy to go into the Down position,

the cue is "Down", not "Lie Down", Get Down",
or anything else... Remember your Pom does not
speak English; he associates the sound of the
word with the action.

- If your Pom is finding an exercise difficult,
  break it down into small steps so it is easier to
  understand.

- Do not make your training sessions boring and
  repetitious; your Pom will simply switch off – or
  bark at you!

- Do not train for too long, particularly with a young
  puppy, who has a very short attention span, and
  always end training sessions on a positive note.

- Above all, have fun so you and your Pom both
  enjoy spending quality time together.

First lessons

A Pom puppy will soak up new experiences like a sponge, so training should start from the time your pup arrives in his new home. It is so much easier to teach good habits rather than trying to correct your puppy when he has established an undesirable pattern of behavior.

Wearing a collar

- An adult Pomeranian has a great mane of hair around his neck, so it may be that he does not wear a collar all the time. But, obviously, there are times when it is essential so it is best to accustom your pup to wearing a soft collar for a few minutes at a time until he gets used to it

- Fit the collar so that you can get at least two fingers between the collar and his neck. Then have a game to distract his attention. This will work for a few moments; then he will stop, put

his back leg up behind his neck and scratch away at the peculiar itchy thing round his neck, which feels so odd.

- Bend down, rotate the collar, pat him on the head and distract him by playing with a toy or giving him a treat. Once he has worn the collar for a few minutes each day, he will soon ignore it and become used to it.

- Remember, never leave the collar on the puppy unsupervised, especially when he is outside in the garden, or when he is in his crate, as it is could get snagged, causing serious injury.

Walking on the leash

- Once your puppy is used to the collar, take him outside into your secure garden where there are no distractions.

- Attach the leash and, to begin with, allow him to wander with the leash trailing, making sure it does not become snagged up. Then pick up the leash and follow the pup where he wants to go; he needs to get used to the sensation of being attached to you.

- The next stage is to get your Pom to follow you, and for this you will need some tasty treats. You can show him a treat in your hand, and then encourage him to follow you. Walk a few paces, and if he is co-operating, stop and reward him. If he puts on the brakes, simply change direction and lure him with the treat.

- Next, introduce changes of direction so your puppy is walking confidently alongside you. At this stage, use a verbal cue "Heel" when your puppy is in the correct position.

- You can then graduate to walking your puppy outside the home – as long as he has completed his vaccination program – starting in quiet areas and building up to busier environments.

- Do not expect too much of your puppy too soon when you are leash walking away from home. He will be distracted by all the new sights and sounds he encounters, so concentrating on leash training will be difficult for him. Give him a chance to look and see, and reward him frequently when he is walking forward confidently on a loose leash.

Come when called

Teaching a reliable recall is invaluable for both you and your Pom. You are secure in the knowledge that he will come back when he is called, and your Pom benefits from being allowed off the leash when he has the freedom to investigate all the exciting new scents he comes across.

We are fortunate that a Pom likes to be with his people, and so he is unlikely to stray too far away. However, he may pick up an extra interesting scent or become distracted by meeting another dog. Obviously, you can allow him a little leeway, but you do want a dog who will come when he is called.

- The breeder may have started this lesson, simply by calling the puppies to "Come" at mealtimes, or when they are moving from one place to another.

- You can build on this when your puppy arrives in his new home, calling him to "Come" when he is in a confined space, such as the kitchen. This is a good place to build up a positive association with the verbal cue – particularly if you ask your puppy to "Come" to get his dinner!

- When your puppy is responding confidently, try calling him when you are in the kitchen and your pup is in another room.

- The next stage is to transfer the lesson to the garden. Arm yourself with some treats, and wait until your puppy is distracted. Then call him, using a higher-pitched, excited tone of voice. At this stage, a puppy wants to be with you, so capitalize on this and keep practicing the verbal cue, and rewarding your puppy with a treat and lots of praise when he comes to you.

- Now you are ready to introduce some distractions. Try calling him when someone else is in the garden, or wait a few minutes until he is investigating a really interesting scent. When he responds, make a really big fuss of him and give him some extra treats so he knows it is worth his while to come to you. If your puppy responds, immediately reward him with a treat.

- If he is slow to come, run away a few steps and then call again, making yourself sound really exciting. Jump up and down, open your arms wide to welcome him; it doesn't matter how silly you look, he needs to see you as the most fun person in the world.

- When you have a reliable recall in the garden, you can venture into the outside world. Do not be too ambitious to begin with; try a recall in a quiet place with the minimum of distractions and only progress to more challenging environments if your Pom is responding well.

- Do not make the mistake of only asking your dog to come at the end of a walk. What is the incentive in coming back to you if all you do is clip on his lead and head for home? Instead, call your dog at random times throughout the walk, giving him a treat and a stroke, and then letting him go free again. In this way, coming to you is always rewarding, and does not signal the end of his free run.

Stationary exercises

The Sit and Down are easy to teach, and mastering these exercises will be rewarding for both you and your Pomeranian.

Sit

The best method is to lure your Pom into position, and for this you can use a treat, a toy, or his food bowl.

- Hold the reward above his head. As he looks up, he will lower his hindquarters and go into a sit.

- Practice this a few times and when your puppy understands what you are asking, introduce the verbal cue "Sit".

- When your Pom understands the exercise, he will respond to the verbal cue alone, and you will not need to reward him every time he sits. However, it is a good idea to give him a treat on a random basis when he co-operates to keep him guessing!

Down

This is an important lesson, and can be a lifesaver if an emergency arises and you need to bring your Pom to an instant halt.

- You can start with your dog in a Sit or a Stand for this exercise. Stand or kneel in front of him and show him you have a treat in your hand. Hold the treat just in front of his nose and slowly lower it towards the ground, between his front legs.

- As your Pom follows the treat he will go down on his front legs and, in a few moments, his hindquarters will follow. Close your hand over the treat so he doesn't cheat and get the treat before he is in the correct position. As soon as he is in the Down, give him the treat and lots of praise.

- Keep practicing, and when your Pom understands what you want, introduce the verbal cue "Down".

Control exercises

These exercises are not the most exciting but they are useful in a variety of different situations. It also teaches your Pom that you are someone to be respected, and if he co-operates, he is always rewarded for making the right decision.

Wait

- This exercise teaches your Pom to "Wait" in position until you give the next command; it differs from the Stay exercise, in which he must stay where you have left him for a more prolonged period. The most useful application of "Wait" is when you are getting your dog out of the car and you need him to stay in position until you clip on his lead.

- Start with your puppy on the lead to give you a greater chance of success. Ask him to "Sit" as you stand in front him. Step back one pace, holding

your hand, palm flat, facing him. Wait a second
and then come back in front of him. You can then
reward him and release him with a word, such as
"OK".

- Practice this a few times, waiting a little longer
before you reward him, and then introduce the
verbal cue "Wait".

- You can reinforce the lesson by using it in different
situations, such as asking your Pom to "Wait"
before you put down his food bowl.

Stay

- You need to differentiate this exercise from
the Wait by using a different hand signal and a
different verbal cue.

- Start with your Pom in the Down as he most likely
to be secure in this position. Stand by his side and
then step forwards, with your hand held back,
palm facing the dog.

- Step back, release him, and then reward him.
Practice until your Pom understands the exercise
and then introduce the verbal cue "Stay".

- Gradually increase the distance you can leave
your puppy, and increase the challenge by walking
around him – and even stepping over him – so that
he learns he must "Stay" until you release him.

Leave

- A response to this verbal cue means that your Pom will learn to give up a toy on request, and it follows on that he will give up anything when he is asked, which is very useful if he has got hold of a forbidden object. You can also use it if you catch him red-handed raiding the bin, or digging up a prized plant in the garden.

- Some Poms can be a little possessive over their toys, and so it is important that your puppy learns that if he gives up something, he will get a reward, which may be even better.

- The "Leave" command can be taught quite easily when you are first playing with your puppy. As you gently take a toy from his mouth, introduce the verbal cue, "Leave", and then praise him.

- If he is reluctant, swap the toy for another toy or a treat. This will usually do the trick.

- Do not try to pull the toy from his mouth if he refuses to give it up, as it will only make him keener to hang on to it. Let the toy go 'dead' in your hand, and then swap it for a new, exciting toy, so this becomes the better option.

- Remember to make a big fuss of your Pom when he co-operates. If he is rewarded with verbal praise, plus a game with a toy or a tasty treat, he will learn that "Leave" is always a good option.

If your Pom has something he values, make sure you swap it with something of equal value so he is prepared to give it up.

Opportunities for Poms

The Pom is an intelligent dog and enjoys the opportunity to use his brain. Despite his small size, you will be surprise at how versatile a Pomeranian can be.

Good Citizen Scheme

The Kennel Club Good Citizen Scheme was introduced to promote responsible dog ownership, and to teach dogs basic good manners. In the US there is one test; in the UK there are four award levels: Puppy Foundation, Bronze, Silver and Gold.

Exercises within the scheme include:

- Walking on leash

- Road walking

- Control at door/gate.

- Recall
- Stay
- Send to bed
- Emergency stop.

Showing

If you plan to exhibit your Pomeranian in the show ring, you will need to be a dedicated groomer to ensure that your dog looks his best when he is inspected by the judge.

You will also need to spend time training your Pom to perform in the show ring. A dog who does not like being handled by the judge, or one that does not walk smartly on the leash, is never going to win high honours, even if he is a top-quality animal. To do well in the ring, a Pom must have that quality that says: "look at me!", which proves that he is a real showman.

In order to prepare your Pom for the busy show atmosphere, you need to work on his socialization, and then take him to ringcraft classes so you both learn what is required in the ring.

Showing at the top level is highly addictive, so watch out! Once you start, you will never have a free date in your diary!

A Pom needs a natural air of showmanship to be successful in the ring.

Agility

The tiny Pomeranian may not seem a natural choice for agility, but those that have taken up the challenge have had a fair degree of success, and clearly get a lot of enjoyment from it.

In this sport, the dog completes an obstacle course under the guidance of his owner. You need a good element of control, as the dog completes the course off the leash.

In competition, each dog completes the course individually and is assessed on both time and accuracy. The dog that completes the course in the fastest time, with the fewest faults, wins the class. The obstacles include an A-frame, a dog-walk, weaving poles, a seesaw, tunnels, and jumps.

Competitive obedience

This is a sport where you are assessed as a dog and handler, completing a series of exercises including heelwork, recalls, retrieves, stays, sendaways and scent discrimination.

The Pom is a quick thinker and likes to please, so he more than capable of learning and performing the exercises. These are relatively simple to begin with, involving heelwork, a recall and stays in the lowest class, and, as your progress through, more exercises

are added, and the aids you are allowed to give are reduced.

To achieve top honours in this discipline requires intensive training as precision and accuracy are of paramount importance.

Heelwork to music

Also known as Canine Freestyle, this activity is becoming increasingly popular. Dog and handler perform a choreographed routine to music, allowing the dog to show off an array of tricks and moves, which delight the crowd. The sparky little Pom has the right personality for this discipline, but you will also need to be pretty light on your feet so you can dance with your petite partner.

The Pom likes to show off, so performing tricks to music will be viewed as the greatest fun.

Health care

We are fortunate that the Pomeranian is generally a healthy dog, so with good routine care, and a well-balanced diet, most dogs will experience few health problems.

However, it is your responsibility to put a program of preventative health care in place – and this should start from the moment your puppy, or older dog, arrives in his new home.

Vaccinations

Dogs are subject to a number of contagious diseases. In the old days, these were killers, and resulted in heartbreak for many owners. Vaccinations have now been developed, and the occurrence of the major infectious diseases is now very rare. However, this will only remain the case if all pet owners follow a strict policy of vaccinating their dogs.

There are vaccinations available for the following diseases:

Canine Adenovirus: This affects the liver; affected dogs have a classic 'blue eye'.

Distemper: A viral disease which causes chest and gastro-intestinal damage. The brain may also be affected, leading to fits and paralysis.

Parvovirus: Causes severe gastro enteritis, and most commonly affects puppies.

Leptospirosis: This bacterial disease is carried by rats and affects many mammals, including humans. It causes liver and kidney damage.

Rabies: A virus that affects the nervous system and is invariably fatal. The first signs are abnormal behavior when the infected dog may bite another animal or a person. Paralysis and death follow. Vaccination is compulsory in most countries. In the UK, dogs traveling overseas must be vaccinated.

Kennel Cough: There are several strains of Kennel Cough, but they all result in a harsh, dry, cough. This disease is rarely fatal; in fact most dogs make a good recovery within a matter of weeks and show few signs of ill health while they are affected. However, kennel cough is highly infectious among dogs that live together so, for this reason, most boarding kennels will insist that your dog is protected by the vaccine, which is given as nose drops.

Lyme Disease: This is a bacterial disease transmitted by ticks (see page 168). The first signs are limping, but the heart, kidneys and nervous system can also be affected. The ticks that transmit the disease occur in specific regions, such as the north-east states of the USA, some of the southern states, California and the upper Mississippi region. Lyme disease is still rare in the UK so vaccinations are not routinely offered.

A puppy is vulnerable to contagious diseases until he has completed his vaccination program.

Vaccination program

In the USA, the American Animal Hospital Association advises vaccination for core diseases, which they list as: distemper, adenovirus, parvovirus and rabies. The requirement for vaccinating for non-core diseases – leptospirosis, lyme disease and kennel cough – should be assessed depending on a dog's individual risk and his likely exposure to the disease.

In the UK, vaccinations are routinely given for distemper, adenovirus, leptospirosis and parvovirus.

In most cases, a puppy will start his vaccinations at around eight weeks of age, with the second part given a fortnight later. However, this does vary depending on the individual policy of your veterinary practice, and the incidence of disease in your area.

You should also talk to your vet about whether to give annual booster vaccinations. This depends on an individual dog's levels of immunity, and how long a particular vaccine remains effective.

Parasites

No matter how well you look after your Pomeranian, you will have to accept that parasites – internal and external – are ever present, and you need to take preventative action.

Internal parasites: As the name suggests, these parasites live inside your dog. Most will find a home in the digestive tract, but there is also a parasite that lives in the heart. If infestation is unchecked, a dog's health will be severely jeopardized, but routine preventative treatment is simple and effective.

External parasites: These parasites live on your dog's body – in his skin and fur, and sometimes in his ears.

Roundworm

This is found in the small intestine, and signs of infestation will be a poor coat, a pot belly, diarrhoea and lethargy. Pregnant mothers should be treated, but it is almost inevitable that the parasites will be passed on to the puppies. For this reason, a breeder will start a worming program, which you will need to continue. Ask your vet for advice on treatment, which will need to continue throughout your dog's life.

Tapeworm

Infestation occurs when fleas and lice are ingested; the adult worm takes up residence in the small intestine, releasing mobile segments (which contain eggs) that can be seen in a dog's feces as small rice-like grains. The only other obvious sign of infestation is irritation of the anus. Again, routine preventative treatment is required throughout your Pom's life.

Heartworm

This parasite is transmitted by mosquitoes, and although it is more present in areas with a warm, humid climate, it is found in all parts of the USA. At present, heartworm is rarely seen in the UK. Preventative treatment should be considered essential, as affected dogs are at risk from heart failure. Dogs living in the USA should also have regular blood tests.

Lungworm

Lungworm is a parasite that lives in the heart and major blood vessels supplying the lungs. The parasite is carried by slugs and snails, and the dog becomes infected when ingesting these, often accidentally when rummaging through undergrowth.

Lungworm is not common, but it is on the increase and a responsible owner should be aware of it.

Fortunately, it is easily preventable and even affected dogs usually make a full recovery if treated early enough. Preventative treatment is required in high-risk areas.

Fleas

A dog may carry dog fleas, cat fleas, and even human fleas. The flea stays on the dog only long enough to have a blood meal and to breed, but its presence will result in itching and scratching. If your dog has an allergy to fleas – which is usually a reaction to the flea's saliva – he will scratch himself until he is raw.

Spot-on treatment, administered on a routine basis, is easy to use and highly effective. You can also treat your dog with a spray or with insecticidal shampoo. Bear in mind that the whole environment your dog lives in will need to be sprayed, and all other pets living in your home will also need to be treated.

How to detect fleas

You may suspect your dog has fleas, but how can you be sure? There are two methods to try.

Run a fine comb through your dog's coat, and see if you can detect the presence of fleas on the skin, or clinging to the comb. Alternatively, sit your dog on some white paper and rub his back. This will dislodge feces from the fleas, which will be visible as small brown specks. To double check, shake the specks on to some damp cotton-wool. Flea feces consists of the dried blood taken from the host, so if the specks turn a lighter shade of red, you know your dog has fleas.

Ticks

These are blood-sucking parasites which are most frequently found in rural areas where sheep or deer are present. The main danger is their ability to pass lyme disease to both dogs and humans.

Lyme disease is prevalent in some areas of the USA (see page 161), although it is still rare in the UK. The treatment you give your dog for fleas generally works for ticks, but you should discuss the best product to use with your vet.

(see page 161)

If your cat has fleas, it will not be long before your Pom has them too.

How to remove a tick

If you spot a tick on your dog, do not try to pluck it off as you risk leaving the hard mouth parts embedded in his skin. The best way to remove a tick is to use a fine pair of tweezers or you can buy a tick remover. Grasp the tick head firmly and then pull the tick straight out from the skin.

If you are using a tick remover, check the instructions, as some recommend a circular twist when pulling. When you have removed the tick, clean the area with mild soap and water.

Ear mites

These parasites live in the outer ear canal. The signs of infestation are a brown, waxy discharge, and your dog will continually shake his head and scratch his ear. If you suspect your Pomeranian has ear mites, a visit to the vet will be needed so that medicated ear drops can be prescribed.

Fur mites

These small, white parasites are visible to the naked eye and are often referred to as 'walking dandruff'. They cause a scurfy coat and mild itchiness. However, they are zoonotic – transferable to humans – so prompt treatment with an insecticide prescribed by your vet is essential.

Harvest mites

These are picked up from the undergrowth, and can be seen as a bright orange patch on the webbing between the toes. This can also be found elsewhere on the body, such as on the ear flaps. Treatment is effective with the appropriate insecticide.

Skin mites

There are two types of parasite that burrow into a dog's skin. *Demodex canis* is transferred from a mother to her pups while they are feeding. Treatment is with a topical preparation, and sometimes antibiotics are needed.

The other skin mite is *sarcoptes scabiei*, which causes intense itching and hair loss. It is highly contagious, so all dogs in a household will need to be treated, which involves repeated bathing with a medicated shampoo.

Common
ailments

As with all living animals, dogs can be affected by a variety of ailments, most of which can be treated effectively after consulting with your vet, who will prescribe appropriate medication and will advise you on how to care for your dog's needs. Here are some of the more common problems that could affect your Pomeranian, with advice on how to deal with them.

Anal glands

These are two small sacs on either side of the anus, which produce a dark-brown secretion that dogs use when they mark their territory. The anal glands should empty every time a dog defecates but, if they become blocked or impacted, a dog will experience increasing discomfort. He may nibble at his rear end, or 'scoot' his bottom along the ground to relieve the irritation.

Treatment involves a trip to the vet, who will empty the glands manually. It is important to do this without delay or infection may occur.

Dental problems

The incidence of dental problems has increased dramatically in recent times and, as highlighted earlier, good dental hygiene will do much to minimize problems with gum infection and tooth decay. If tartar accumulates to the extent that you cannot remove it by brushing, the vet will need to intervene. In a situation such as this, an anesthetic will need to be administered so the tartar can be removed manually.

Diarrhoea

There are many reasons why a dog has diarrhoea, but most commonly it is the result of scavenging, a sudden change of diet, or an adverse reaction to a particular type of food.

If your Pom is suffering from diarrhoea, the first step is to withdraw food for a day. It is important that he does not dehydrate, so make sure that fresh drinking water is available. However, drinking too much can increase the diarrhoea, which may be accompanied with vomiting, so limit how much he drinks at any one time.

After allowing the stomach to rest, feed a bland diet, such as white fish or chicken with boiled rice, for a few days. In most cases, your dog's motions will return to normal and you can resume normal feeding, although this should be done gradually.

However, if this fails to work and the diarrhoea persists for more than a few days, you should consult you vet. Your dog may have an infection, which needs to be treated with antibiotics, or the diarrhoea may indicate some other problem that needs expert diagnosis.

Ear infections

The Pomeranian has small, erect ears that allow air to circulate freely, which minimizes potential ear infections. However, it is important to check your Pom's ears on a routine basis.

A healthy ear is clean, with no sign of redness or inflammation, and no evidence of a waxy brown discharge or a foul odor. If you see your dog scratching his ear, shaking his head, or holding one ear at an odd angle, you will need to consult your vet.

The most likely causes are ear mites (see page 170), an infection, or there may a foreign body, such as a grass seed, trapped in the ear.

Depending on the cause, treatment is with medicated eardrops, possibly containing antibiotics. If a foreign body is suspected, the vet will need to carry our further investigations.

Eye problems

The Pom's eyes are set well into his skull; they do not protrude, as in breeds such as the Pug, so they are not vulnerable to injury.

However, if your Pom's eyes look red and sore, he may be suffering from conjunctivitis. This may, or may not be accompanied with a watery or a crusty discharge. Conjunctivitis can be caused by a bacterial or viral infection, it could be the result of an injury, or it could be an adverse reaction to pollen.

You will need to consult your vet for a correct diagnosis, but in the case of an infection, treatment with medicated eye drops is effective.

In some instances, a dog may suffer from dry, itchy eye, which he may further injure through scratching. This condition, known as *keratoconjunctivitis sicca*, may be inherited.

Foreign bodies

In the home, puppies – and some older dogs – cannot resist chewing anything that looks interesting.

The toys you choose for your dog should be suitably robust to withstand damage, but children's toys can be irresistible. Some dogs will chew – and swallow – anything from socks, tights, and other items from the laundry basket, to golf balls and stones from the garden. Obviously, these items are indigestible and could cause an obstruction in your dog's intestine, which is potentially lethal.

The signs to look for are vomiting, and a tucked up posture. The dog will often be restless and will look as though he is in pain. In this situation, you must get your dog to the vet without delay, as surgery will be needed to remove the obstruction.

The other type of foreign body that may cause problems is grass seed. A grass seed can enter an orifice such as a nostril, down an ear, the gap between the eye and the eyelid, or penetrate the soft skin between the toes. It can also be swallowed.

The introduction of a foreign body induces a variety of symptoms, depending on the point of entry and its final location. The signs to look for include head shaking/ear scratching, the eruption of an abscess, sore, inflamed eyes, or a persistent cough. The vet will be able to make a proper diagnosis, and surgery may be required.

Heatstroke

On hot days, make sure your Pomeranian always has access to shady areas, and wait for a cooler part of the day before going for a walk. Be extra careful if you leave your Pom in the car, as the temperature can rise dramatically - even on a cloudy day. Heatstroke can happen very rapidly, and unless you are able lower your dog's temperature, it can be fatal.

If your Pomeranian appears to be suffering from heatstroke, lie him flat and try to reduce his core body temperature by wrapping him in cool towels. A dog should not be immersed in cold water as this will cause the blood vessels to constrict, impeding heat dissipation. As soon as he made some recovery, take him to the vet, where cold intravenous fluids can be administered.

Lameness/limping

There are a wide variety of reasons why a dog can go lame, from a simple muscle strain to a fracture, ligament damage, or more complex problems with the joints which may be an inherited disorder (see page 184). It takes an expert to make a correct diagnosis, so if you are concerned about your dog, do not delay in seeking help.

As your Pomeranian becomes elderly, he may suffer from arthritis, which you will see as general stiffness, particularly when he gets up after resting. It will help if you ensure his bed is in a warm, draught-free location, and, if your Pom gets wet after exercise, you must dry him thoroughly.

If your elderly Pom seems to be in pain, consult your vet, who will be able to help with pain relief medication.

Skin problems

If your dog is scratching or nibbling at his skin, the first thing to check for is fleas (see page 168). There are other external parasites that cause itching and hair loss, but you will need a vet to help you find the culprit.

An allergic reaction is another major cause of skin problems. It can be quite an undertaking to find the cause of the allergy, and you will need to follow your vet's advice, which often requires eliminating specific ingredients from the diet, as well as looking at environmental factors.

Inherited disorders

Like all pedigree dogs, the Pomeranian does have a few breed-related disorders. If diagnosed with any of the diseases listed below, it is important to remember that they can affect offspring so breeding from affected dogs should be discouraged.

There are now recognized screening tests to enable breeders to check for affected individuals and hence reduce the prevalence of these diseases within the breed.

DNA testing is also becoming more widely available, and as research into the different genetic diseases progresses, more DNA tests are being developed.

Alopecia X

This condition, also known as black skin disease, refers to hair loss, accompanied by darkening of the skin, known as hyperpigmentation. As with many

skin conditions, it can be the result of differing factors.

Alopecia X is thought to be an X-linked inherited disorder as it affects more females than males. It also has a higher incidence among the spitz breeds. Hair loss generally starts at the base of the tail or the lower chest and then affects the inner thighs spreading along the back and up the tail.

The condition is purely cosmetic but it is obviously upsetting for owners. There are a number of treatments which your vet can prescribe, but this tends to be on a trial and error basis as the underlying cause of the condition is unknown.

Collapsing trachea

This is the result of a malformation of the windpipe, causing the airway to collapse, thereby restricting airflow into the lungs. It is often characterized by a honking cough, and is more evident when a Pom is excited, or when he is pulling against his collar. In some cases, a Pom may cough when he tries to eat or drink. Treatment is needed to suppress the cough and inflammation. Using a harness rather than a collar is also recommended.

Cryptorchidism

This hereditary condition can occur in any male dog, and although it is very far from being widespread in Pomeranians, it is worth asking for a male puppy to be checked by the vet on his first visit.

Both testicles (testes) should be present in the scrotum at the time a puppy is purchased. If they do not descend from the abdomen by adulthood, the dog is described as unilaterally cryptorchid (one testes retained) or bilaterally cryptorchid (both retained).

This obviously affects a dog's breeding potential, but even if you have no plans to breed, it is recommended that the testes are surgically removed to prevent further problems.

Heart murmurs

These are most often discovered when a puppy has his first health check on vaccination.

The vet will be able to grade the heart murmur, which can range from mild to severe. In addition, there is a so-called 'innocent' murmur, which will generally disappear by adulthood.

Hypoglycemia

This is a life-threatening condition that is more likely to affect Toy breeds. It involves a sudden drop in blood sugar, and the signs are disorientation, loss of balance, shivering and muscle tremors, escalating to loss of consciousness and coma. Veterinary attention should be sought without delay.

Hypothyroidism

This occurs when the thyroid gland fails to produce sufficient amounts of thyroid hormone. This results in a slowing of the metabolism, and the most common signs are hair loss, lethargy, weight gain, joint pain and skins problems.

The condition can be diagnosed through blood tests and treatment by medication is usually effective.

Patellar luxation

This is a condition in which the kneecap (patella) slips out of place or dislocates. The kneecap moves in a groove at the lower end of the femur (thigh bone). Some dogs – mostly small and Toy breeds – are born with a groove that is not deep enough to retain the kneecap so that it pops out of its groove.

Surgery may be needed in severe cases but generally a Pom will live with this condition and be largely unaffected, although arthritis may occur in the stifle in later life.

Summing up

It may give the pet owner cause for concern to find about health problems that may affect their dog. But it is important to bear in mind that acquiring some basic knowledge is an asset, as it will allow you to spot signs of trouble at an early stage. Early diagnosis is very often the means to the most effective treatment.

Fortunately, the Pomeranian is a generally healthy and disease-free dog with his only visits to the vet being annual check-ups. In most cases, owners can look forward to enjoying many happy years with this loyal companion.

Useful addresses

Please contact your Kennel Club to obtain contact information about breed clubs in your area.

UK
The Kennel Club (UK)
1 Clarges Street London, W1J 8AB
Telephone: 0870 606 6750
Fax: 0207 518 1058
Web: www.thekennelclub.org.uk

USA
American Kennel Club (AKC)
5580 Centerview Drive, Raleigh, NC 27606.
Telephone: 919 233 9767
Fax: 919 233 3627
Email: info@akc.org
Web: www.akc.org

United Kennel Club (UKC)
100 E Kilgore Rd, Kalamazoo,
MI 49002-5584, USA.
Tel: 269 343 9020
Fax: 269 343 7037
Web: www.ukcdogs.com

Australia
Australian National Kennel Council (ANKC)
The Australian National Kennel Council is the administrative body for pure breed canine affairs in Australia. It does not, however, deal directly with dog exhibitors, breeders or judges. For information pertaining to breeders, clubs or shows, please contact the relevant State or Territory Body.

International
Fédération Cynologique Internationalé (FCI)
Place Albert 1er, 13, B-6530 Thuin, Belgium.
Tel: +32 71 59.12.38
Fax: +32 71 59.22.29
Web: www.fci.be

Training and behavior
UK
Association of Pet Dog Trainers
Telephone: 01285 810811
Web: www.apdt.co.uk

Canine Behaviour
Association of Pet Behaviour Counsellors
Telephone: 01386 751151
Web: www.apbc.org.uk

USA
Association of Pet Dog Trainers
Tel: 1 800 738 3647
Web: www.apdt.com

American College of Veterinary Behaviorists
Web: www.dacvb.org

American Veterinary Society of Animal Behavior
Web: www.avsabonline.org

Australia
APDT Australia Inc
Web: www.apdt.com.au

For details of regional behaviorists, contact the relevant State or Territory Controlling Body.

Activities

UK
Agility Club
www.agilityclub.co.uk

British Flyball Association
Telephone: 01628 829623
Web: www.flyball.org.uk

USA
North American Dog Agility Council
Web: www.nadac.com

North American Flyball Association, Inc.
Tel/Fax: 800 318 6312
Web: www.flyball.org

Australia
Agility Dog Association of Australia
Tel: 0423 138 914
Web: www.adaa.com.au

NADAC Australia
Web: www.nadacaustralia.com

Australian Flyball Association
Tel: 0407 337 939
Web: www.flyball.org.au

International
World Canine Freestyle Organisation
Tel: (718) 332-8336
Web: www.worldcaninefreestyle.org

Health

UK
British Small Animal Veterinary Association
Tel: 01452 726700
Web: www.bsava.com

Royal College of Veterinary Surgeons
Tel: 0207 222 2001
Web: www.rcvs.org.uk

www.dogbooksonline.co.uk/healthcare

Alternative Veterinary Medicine Centre
Tel: 01367 710324
Web: www.alternativevet.org

USA
American Veterinary Medical Association
Tel: 800 248 2862
Web: www.avma.org

American College of Veterinary Surgeons
Tel: 301 916 0200
Toll Free: 877 217 2287
Web: www.acvs.org

Canine Eye Registration Foundation
The Veterinary Medical DataBases
1717 Philo Rd, PO Box 3007,
Urbana, IL 61803-3007
Tel: 217-693-4800
Fax: 217-693-4801
Web: www.vmdb.org/cerf.html

Orthopedic Foundation of Animals
2300 E Nifong Boulevard
Columbia, Missouri, 65201-3806
Tel: 573 442-0418
Fax: 573 875-5073
Web: www.offa.org

American Holistic Veterinary Medical
Association
Tel: 410 569 0795
Web: www.ahvma.org

Australia
Australian Small Animal Veterinary
Association
Tel: 02 9431 5090
Web: www.asava.com.au

Australian Veterinary Association
Tel: 02 9431 5000
Web: www.ava.com.au

Australian College Veterinary Scientists
Tel: 07 3423 2016
Web: www.acvsc.org.au

Australian Holistic Vets
Web: www.ahv.com.au